Fact Finders®

ENGINEERING WONDERS

THE GREAT WALL OF CHINA

BY REBECCA STANBOROUGH

raintree

a Capstone company — publishers for children

Raintree is an imprint of Capstone Global Library Limited, a company incorporated in England and Wales having its registered office at 264 Banbury Road, Oxford, OX27DY – Registered company number: 6695582

www.raintree.co.uk
myorders@raintree.co.uk

Edited by Elizabeth Johnson and Gena Chester
Designed by Veronica Scott
Picture research by Svetlana Zhurkin
Production by Lori Barbeau
Originated by Capstone Global Library Limited
Printed and bound in China.

ISBN 978 1 4747 1179 1
20 19 18 17 16
10 9 8 7 6 5 4 3 2 1

British Library Cataloguing in Publication Data
A full catalogue record for this book is available from the British Library.

Acknowledgements
We would like to thank the following for permission to reproduce photographs: Alamy: Daniel Palmer, 13; Bridgeman Images: Look and Learn/Private Collection/Mongol Soldiers Breaking Through the Great Wall of China, Doughty, C.L. (1913-85), 17; Capstone Press, 12; Dreamstime: Ming Xu, 26—27; Getty Images: Travel Ink, 20; Image from The Great Wall of China 221 BC-AD 1644, by Stephen Turnbull, © Osprey Publishing Ltd., cover; National Geographic Creative: Hsien-Min Yang, 11; North Wind Picture Archives, 6—7, 8, 9; Shutterstock: 1970s, 24 (inset), hecke61, 16, imageshunter, 5, Mikhail Nekrasov, 24 (bottom), Mila May, 18—19, 22, sihasakprachum, 15, tisskananat, 21, wizdata, 29, Yuri Yavnik, 23; Wikimedia: The Real Bear, 14.

Design elements: Shutterstock.

Every effort has been made to contact copyright holders of materials reproduced in this book. Any omissions will be rectified in subsequent printings if notice is given to the publisher.

All the internet addresses (URLs) given in this book were valid at the time of going to press. However, due to the dynamic nature of the internet, some addresses may have been changed, or sites may have changed or ceased to exist since publication. While the author and publisher regret any inconvenience this may cause readers, no responsibility for any such changes can be accepted by either the author or the publisher.

CONTENTS

CHAPTER 1

THE EARTH DRAGON

The Great Wall of China is the largest defence structure ever built. It travels over mountains, across rivers and through deserts. It is studded with forts, towers and gateways. It has inspired myths, poems, art and music. But the Great Wall of China is not really a single wall.

What the Chinese people call *wan li chang cheng*, the long wall of ten-thousand miles, is really many walls. The walls were built in different regions of the large country, using different materials. Each wall was built to protect China from invaders. Over time, sections of walls were connected. The Great Wall was built over a span of more than 2,000 years. The **engineering** designs and methods changed greatly over that period of time.

engineering use of science and mathematics to design, build or maintain machines, buildings or public works

4

Today, many people refer to the Great Wall as an "earth dragon" because of the way it winds across the landscape of China. In some places it is a wide and mighty fortress. In others, it is no more than a slight swelling of the ground. Each part of China's Great Wall is the result of the hard work and engineering skills of many generations of Chinese people.

Did you know?

It used to be thought that the Great Wall of China was about 8,850 kilometres (5,500 miles) long. But in 2012 a new study found that the Great Wall is more than 21,000 kilometres (13,000 miles) long.

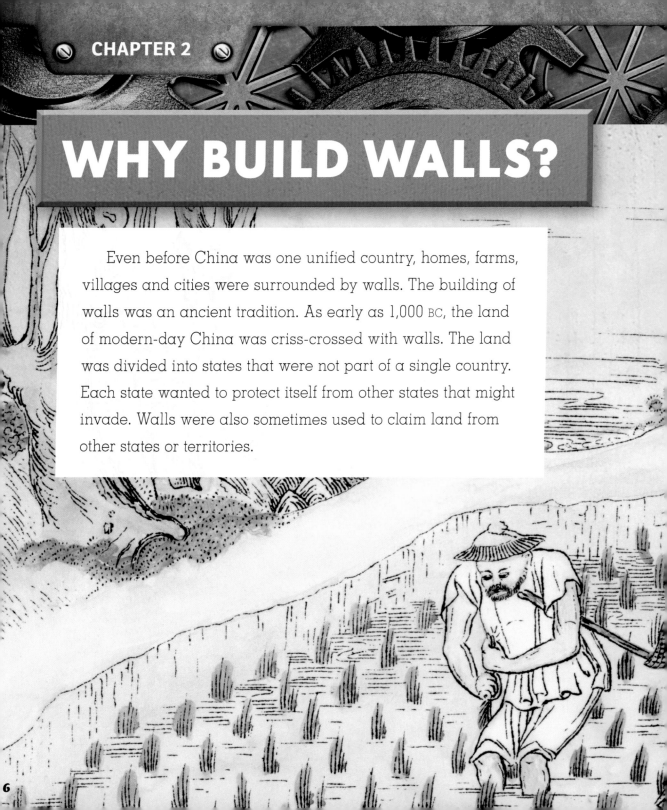

CHAPTER 2

WHY BUILD WALLS?

Even before China was one unified country, homes, farms, villages and cities were surrounded by walls. The building of walls was an ancient tradition. As early as 1,000 BC, the land of modern-day China was criss-crossed with walls. The land was divided into states that were not part of a single country. Each state wanted to protect itself from other states that might invade. Walls were also sometimes used to claim land from other states or territories.

TRADE OR INVADE?

Thousands of years ago, most of the people living in the heartland of China were farmers. They lived in settled communities. In the steppe region to the north of modern-day China, the land was dry and grassy. It was not good for farming, but it was very good for grazing herds of animals. So pastoral nomads moved from place to place. The nomads of the steppe were another threat to Chinese states.

Often, farmers and nomads traded peacefully. But when trade was cut off, the nomads raided Chinese villages. They took what they needed by force. Many historians think people from the Chinese states also rode north. They took land from the nomads. The Chinese and the people of the north tried many ways to find peace. When all else failed, the Chinese people built walls.

Pastoral nomads are groups that raise livestock and move within their established territory to find good pastures for their animals.

nomad invaders attacking Chinese territory

CHAPTER 3

A WALL FOR UNIFIED CHINA

A man called Yin Zheng unified China into a single nation in 221 BC. He renamed himself Qin Shihuangdi, which means First **Emperor** of the Qin **Dynasty**.

As emperor, Qin Shihuangdi was a **tyrant**. He murdered people who challenged him. He burned books and buried scholars alive. He forced his people to work on large building projects. Hundreds of thousands of people built roads, palaces and canals for their emperor.

Qin Shihuangdi ordered his general, Meng Tian, to connect the old state walls into one long barrier. During his short reign, China's first emperor connected more than 5,000 kilometres (about 3,000 miles) of walls. The workers carried out back-breaking labour on rough terrain in all kinds of weather.

dynasty period of time during which a country's rulers all come from one family
emperor male ruler of an empire; Chinese emperors made all the decisions for the people they ruled
tyrant someone who rules other people in a cruel or unjust way

THE LEGEND OF LADY MENG JIANG

The Great Wall is at the heart of one of China's oldest myths: "Meng Jiang, the common woman who brought down the wall with her tears". According to the legend, Meng Jiang's husband was forced to travel far away to work on the wall. For many months, she heard nothing from him. Meng Jiang made up her mind to take him warm clothes for the winter. When she arrived at the wall, she was too late. Her husband had died. Meng Jiang wept so much that her tears flooded the wall. The wall crumbled, revealing her husband's bones.

Did you know?

As many as 400,000 people died building the long wall. Some people call it "the longest cemetery in the world".

HOW WERE THE QIN WALLS MADE?

General Meng Tian built the Qin wall using an ancient tradition called *hangtu*, which is also called "rammed-earth" construction. First, workers dug a ditch and poured in pebbles to make a foundation. A set of fences were put on either side of the foundation. The fences were made of wooden poles. The wood often came from poplar trees. Workers filled the space between the fences with a layer of yellow soil called loess.

Workers pounded the loess until it was packed down. They used wooden poles with stone or wooden blocks fixed to the ends. On top of the tamped layer, they laid thin stalks of bamboo to allow air to circulate and dry the earth. Then more layers of loess were added and pounded until they reached the top of the wooden frame. Sometimes the frame was removed and sometimes it was left in place. The tamped-earth wall could be up to 6 metres (19 feet) high. Meng Tian also used the dangerous cliffs and steep mountains of the region. During the Qin era, the wall builders let this fierce terrain act as a barrier.

Over many centuries, time and weather slowly eroded the tamped-earth walls. Today, almost nothing is left of the Qin-era long wall.

FAST FACTS ABOUT RAMMED-EARTH CONSTRUCTION

- *Hangtu* is one of the oldest building methods on Earth. There is evidence of rammed-earth buildings from 5,000 BC.

- Workers know the walls are ready by the sounds their tools make. When the soil is first pounded, it makes a dull thud. When the earth has been pounded enough, the tool makes a ringing sound.

- The walls are ready to bear weight as soon as the tamping is complete. The walls continue to harden and set for up to two years afterwards. This hardening time is called curing.

- Rammed-earth walls are almost as strong as concrete. They are also able to withstand great heat.

- If bamboo reinforces the walls, they can even withstand earthquakes.

a modern-day rammed-earth house

CHAPTER 4

STICKS AND STONES

Qin Shihuangdi ruled for just 36 years. The Han Dynasty that followed ruled for 400 years. The Han tried to make peace with the northern nomads. They sent thousands of families to live in the border lands. The Han also extended Chinese territory to the west along the silk trade routes. Under the Han, the wall stretched all the way to the Gobi Desert. How were Han walls different?

This tower from the Han era overlooks the Gobi Desert.

Like the Qin-era builders, the Han made tamped-earth walls. In the desert region, however, the soil was much looser. It contained many small pebbles. The Han added red willow and reeds to the soil. This made the desert walls stronger. When the earth had been well pounded, they coated the entire wall with oily clay. The wall looked smooth and yellow.

During the Han Dynasty, builders also made stacked stone walls. They cut large **granite** stones from nearby **quarries** and carried them to the building sites. They used tools to shape the stones so they would fit together. **Masons** trimmed and set small stones between the larger ones to hold them in place without **mortar**. These walls could also reach up to 6 metres (19 feet) in height.

granite hard rock used in building; igneous rock with visible crystals; generally composed of feldspar, mica and quartz

quarry place where stone or other minerals are dug from the ground

mason skilled worker who builds by laying units of strong material such as stone or brick

mortar cement-like mixture used in construction that, once hardened, binds together bricks and stones

CHAPTER 5

BRICKS AND STONES

For centuries, Chinese dynasties repaired or extended sections of the wall. Sometimes they ignored the wall. The walls worked to keep out some invaders, but not all of them. Walls proved no match for the armies led by Kublai Khan. When Kublai Khan overthrew the Song Dynasty emperor in AD 1279, he killed thousands of Chinese people. One song from the era translates as:

> *The wall was built with cries of pain and sadness;*
> *The moon and the Milky Way seem low in comparison with it.*
> *But if all the white bones of the dead had been left piled up there,*
> *They would reach the same height as the wall.*

Kublai Khan's forces taking over the wall

Eventually, Khan's dynasty was overthrown. A peasant called Zhu Yuanzhang began the Ming Dynasty. The Ming Dynasty built the parts of the Great Wall that are well known around the world. Many sections of the older walls wore down over time or were taken apart. The Ming walls are the best preserved and most visited today.

Did you know?

Kublai Khan is the grandson of the famous Mongol warrior Genghis Khan.

MING WALLS

Chinese citizens worked on the Ming wall for over two centuries. In the west, the wall was built of tamped earth, just as it had been in the past. But in the east, the workers used stone and brick. Building a stone and brick wall meant thousands more workers were needed. Soldiers, poor people and criminals were all brought to the wall to work. Many people did not have a choice.

The Jinshanling section of the Ming-era wall is known for its dramatic zigzag pattern, called switch-backs.

Walls of the Ming era were wide and strong. They consisted of an outer wall, an inner wall and a layer of tamped filler in between them. The filler was a mixture of loess, sand and pebbles. Some parts of the Ming wall are so wide that five horses could ride side by side along the top.

A wall of this size needed a firm foundation. In some places, volcanic **bedrock** formed the base of the wall. In other places, skilled stonemasons installed large granite stones. The base of the wall was wider at the bottom to make it more stable. Lower parts of the wall were made of stone. Upper parts of the wall were often made of brick.

bedrock layer of solid rock beneath the layers of soil and loose gravel broken up by weathering

MAKING A MING BRICK

Ming bricks were larger than the bricks we use to build houses today. They were also much stronger. Ming masons covered their dome-shaped **kilns** with dirt. They slowly baked the bricks at high temperatures. Bricks baked for seven days. Then masons poured water over the kilns to cool them. This made the bricks stronger.

The mortar used to "glue" the bricks in place was made of **lime** and clay. Modern scientists have found all sorts of other ingredients in the mortar of the Great Wall. They have found leaves, egg whites, fish oil and even animal blood.

kiln hot oven used to fire clay; small kilns fire pottery and art; large kilns bake many bricks or tiles at once

lime white substance made by heating limestone or shells and used in making plaster and cement and in farming

Oxen, donkeys and humans carried the bricks to the building site in carts, baskets or wheelbarrows. If the path to the wall was too steep, a human chain was organized. The bricks were passed from hand to hand up the hill.

Builders attached drainage spouts to the walls. This kept rain from seeping into the bricks. The spouts emptied inside the wall. The builders did not want to water the ground on the outside of the wall. If trees and shrubs grew on the outside, invaders might use them to climb onto the wall.

THE SECRET INGREDIENT IN CHINESE MORTAR

Recently scientists looked closely at the ingredients in the mortar that holds parts of the Great Wall together. They discovered something surprising – sticky rice! When Chinese builders added sweet rice soup to the mortar, they created a stronger bond than mortar made without the rice. A carbohydrate in the rice, called amylopectin, makes the grains of lime smaller. Mortar packed tight with small grains is better for keeping out water and weather. The sticky rice mortar is so strong that walls made with it have resisted powerful earthquakes. Even bulldozers have not been able to knock down some of the walls made with rice mortar!

CHAPTER 6

FORTIFICATIONS

The Great Wall is more than a solid expanse of stone and brick. It has towers, gatehouses, courtyards and bridges. If the physical barrier of the wall couldn't keep out invaders, the soldiers working and living at the Great Wall were there to fight and send warnings of the invasions. They also used the wall to move troops and goods across the land. The Great Wall's **fortifications** are part of what makes it such a wonder.

The wall's notches, called crenellations, allowed guards to shoot at raiders.

TOWERS

There are thousands of towers along the Great Wall. Some are small. Some are as large as forts or castles. Many of the towers are not connected to the wall at all.

When a tower is part of the wall, the wall itself usually forms the tower floor. Upper storeys and colourful roof tiles were common on Ming-era towers. Larger towers could be used to store food and weapons in case of a **siege**. The only way in to some towers was a ladder that could be pulled up during an attack.

fortifications building or walls built as military defences

siege attack on a castle, fort or other enclosed location; a siege is usually meant to force the people inside the enclosed location to give up

Soldiers often lived in the towers. They watched for invading forces. In places where attacks happened frequently, towers were set as close as thirty paces from each other.

If a guard saw troops coming, he could warn other outposts. At night, signal fires were used to communicate with other posts. During the day, soldiers signalled with smoke.

PASSES

Some sections of the wall run through steep mountain ranges. On the peaks, the wall is narrow – sometimes just 50 centimetres (19 inches) wide. Bricks were laid **parallel** to the slope of the mountain to make it easier to build the wall. Labourers carried granite and pounded earth on these mountaintops. The air was thin and breathing must have been difficult. Some portions of the wall were built 1,980 metres (6,500 feet) above sea level!

Low points in mountain ranges are called passes. The Great Wall acted as a gateway through the mountain passes. On the inside of the wall, wide ramps made it easy for troops to carry up supplies. It was much harder to enter from the other side of the wall. Gatehouses were built so that visitors had to travel under the wall, with guards posted overhead. Visitors passed into walled courtyards with tricky turns engineered to slow them down.

parallel in a straight line and an equal distance apart

Jiayuguan, where Sangui let the Manchu prince enter, guards the Shanhai Pass at the western end of the wall.

DID THE WALL WORK?

Throughout the 2,000 years that the Great Wall was being built, sometimes it kept out invaders and sometimes it did not. Even though many of the walls were connected over time, invaders often went around sections that were not connected.

The wall built during the Ming era was expensive and beautiful. But like the other walls before it, the Ming wall failed to keep out invaders. The Ming Dynasty ended in 1644 when General Wu Sangui opened the gates and a Manchu prince entered China.

CHAPTER 7

THE WALL IN MODERN TIMES

In time, the dynasty founded by the Manchu prince also fell. The wall was no longer used as an important part of military strategy. From 1933 to 1945, however, it played a brief, but vital, role in helping China defeat Japan in the Sino-Japanese War.

Today, thousands of tourists trek up and down the worn steps of the Great Wall every year. Foreign leaders pose for pictures at the forts. **Archaeologists** work to restore the crumbling sections in remote regions.

The Great Wall of China is not one but *many* earth dragons made of tamped earth, stone and brick. As they travel over plains and through mountains, the dragons tell the long story of the Chinese people who planned and built the *wan li chang cheng* piece by piece over 2,000 years.

archaeologist person who studies how people lived in the past

GLOSSARY

archaeologist person who studies how people lived in the past

bedrock layer of solid rock beneath the layers of soil and loose gravel broken up by weathering

dynasty period of time during which a country's rulers all come from one family

emperor male ruler of an empire; Chinese emperors made all the decisions for the people they ruled

engineering use of science and mathematics to design, build or maintain machines, buildings or public works

fortifications buildings or walls built as military defences

granite hard rock used in building; igneous rock with visible crystals; generally composed of feldspar, mica and quartz

kiln hot oven used to fire clay; small kilns fire pottery and art; large kilns bake many bricks or tiles at once

lime white substance made by heating limestone or shells and used in making plaster and cement and in farming

mason skilled worker who builds by laying units of strong material such as stone or brick

mortar cement-like mixture used in construction that, once hardened, binds together bricks and stones

parallel in a straight line and an equal distance apart

quarry place where stone or other minerals are dug from the ground

siege attack on a castle, fort or other enclosed location; a siege is usually meant to force the people inside the enclosed location to give up

tyrant someone who rules other people in a cruel or unjust way

BOOKS

Ancient China (DK Eyewitness Books), Arthur Cotterell (DK Publishing, 2005)

China (Countries Around the World), Patrick Catel (Raintree, 2013)

Chinese Myths and Legends (All About Myths), Anita Ganeri (Raintree, 2013)

Daily Life in Shang Dynasty China (Daily Life in Ancient Civilizations), Lori Hile (Raintree, 2015)

WEBSITES

www.bbc.co.uk/schools/primaryhistory/worldhistory/tang_tomb_figures/
Find out more about the history of China, and its first emperor.

www.dkfindout.com/uk/history/ancient-china/great-wall-china/
Take a closer look at the Great Wall of China.

COMPREHENSION QUESTIONS

1. Qin Shihuangdi can be viewed as a terrible leader. Give evidence from the text that supports this view.

2. By some measures, Qin Shihuangdi was also a great leader. Give evidence from the text to support this claim.

3. The author tells the tale of Meng Jiang, the woman whose tears crumbled the Great Wall. How does this folk tale reflect the reality of what workers and their families experienced during the building of the Great Wall?

INDEX